HOW ARE YOU?: FIRST WORDS BABY BOOK

Speedy Publishing LLC
40 E. Main St. #1156
Newark, DE 19711
www.speedypublishing.com

BALL

CANDY

DOG

CAT & FiSH

HOUSE

LEAF

BOOK

CRAYON

KiDS

EGGS

RIBBON

FISH

APPLE

BLOCKS

PUPPY

POT

CARDS

FACE

DOOR

GiFTS

MOUSE

FIRE

EAT

PLAY

RUN

PHONE

FORK

PILLOW

LEMON

www.ingramcontent.com/pod-product-compliance
Lightning Source LLC
LaVergne TN
LVHW060515170826
845677LV00026B/1762

* 9 7 9 8 8 6 9 4 5 4 3 3 1 *